GEOGRAPHY SKILLS

Understanding
LANDFORMS

Barbara Taylor

Smart Apple Media

This book has been published in cooperation with Franklin Watts.

Editor: Jennifer Schofield
Consultant: Steve Watts
(FRGS, Principal Lecturer University of Sunderland)
Art director: Jonathan Hair
Design: Mo Choy
Artwork: Ian Thompson
Picture researcher: Kathy Lockley

Acknowledgements:
Altitude/Still Pictures 15. Jacques Descloitres, MOBIS Land Rapid Response Team/NASA/GSFC 27. Michael & Patricia Fogden/Minden/Frank Lane Picture Agency 29. Michael Graber/Still Pictures 13. David T. Grewcock/Frank Lane Picture Agency 19. Robert Harding Picture Library 21, 22, 37, 38. Ian Harwood/Ecoscene 24. Dennis Johnson/Lonely Planet Images 16. c.Andrew K/epa/epa/Corbis 33. Chris Knapton/Science Photo Library 6. Wayne Lawler/Ecoscene 41. Alberto Nardi/NHPA 11. Mark Newman/Frank Lane Picture Agency 3b, 35, Cover. Fritz Polking/Ecoscene 25. c.Reuters/Corbis 32. Kevin Schafer/NHPA 8. Erik Schaffer/Ecoscene 43. c. Dennis Scott/Corbis 3t, 4/5, 44/5, 46/7, Cover. Bob Watkins/Photofusion 40. Martin Wendler/NHPA 30. David Woodfall/Still Pictures 42.

Published in the United States by Smart Apple Media
2140 Howard Drive West, North Mankato, Minnesota 56003

Printed in the United States, in North Mankato, MN
090309
1189

Library of Congress Cataloging-in-Publication Data

Taylor, Barbara, 1954–
Understanding landforms / by Barbara Taylor.
p. cm. — (Geography skills)
Includes index.
ISBN-13: 978-1-59920-049-1
1. Landforms—Juvenile literature. 2. Physical geography—Juvenile literature. I. Title.

GB402.T39 2007
551.41—dc22   2006036141

9 8 7 6 5 4 3

Contents

What shapes the land?

Landforms are natural features such as cliffs or volcanoes on the earth's surface. They are caused by powerful forces deep inside the earth and by wind and water carving the land surface into new shapes. Understanding the shape of the land helps people survive floods, earthquakes, and other natural disasters. It also helps people plan building projects, protect water supplies, and decide on sustainable ways of using the land that will protect it for the future.

Understanding landforms helps people build roads and other structures in the right place. They, in turn, change the shape of the land.

crust

mantle

outer core

inner core

CHANGING SHAPE

The shape of the land is changing all the time. Heat rising from the hot center, or core, of the earth pushes the surface up into mountains and causes volcanoes to erupt. It also moves land on the surface of the earth sideways and tears it apart. On the surface, wind and water wear away the land in some places and build it up in others.

These contour lines help people visualize the shape of the land using a map.

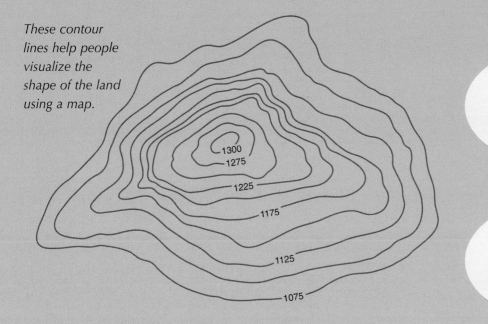

1300
1275
1225
1175
1125
1075

HOW HIGH IS THE LAND?

You can find out more about the ups and downs of the land by drawing a line graph using a map. On a map, thin brown lines connect places that are the same height above sea level. These brown lines are called contour lines. If the contour lines are close together, the land is steep and hilly.

Using the sample of contours above, trace the contour lines onto a piece of tracing paper. Turn the drawing over, place it on top of a blank piece of paper, and firmly rub over the lines with a soft pencil to transfer them to the paper. Mark the height above sea level on each contour.

Now, draw a graph like the example below, but use your measurements.

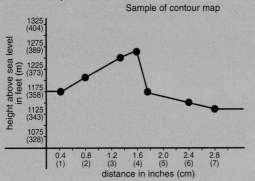

Sample of contour map

height above sea level in feet (m)

1325 (404)
1275 (389)
1225 (373)
1175 (358)
1125 (343)
1075 (328)

0.4 (1)   0.8 (2)   1.2 (3)   1.6 (4)   2.0 (5)   2.4 (6)   2.8 (7)

distance in inches (cm)

Use a ruler to draw a straight line across the middle of your contour lines. On the line graph, plot the point where each contour line crosses the straight line. When you connect the points, you should be able to see the shape of the land as if you were standing in the country looking at it. Use the scale on the map to determine how large the hill is. Look at some contour maps of your local area. Try to visualize the shape of the land by studying the pattern of the contour lines.

KEY SKILLS

Throughout this book, you will learn different skills. Each different skill is represented by one of the following icons:

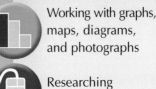

Completing a practical activity

Analyzing information

Working with graphs, maps, diagrams, and photographs

Looking at global issues

Researching information

Observing

Earth's jigsaw

The surface, or crust, of the earth is broken into huge plates that fit together like the pieces of a jigsaw. Most of the plates include some large areas of land, or continents, and some areas of ocean.

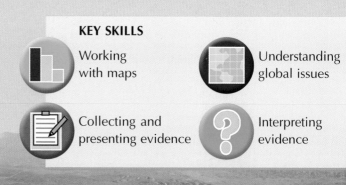

CONTINENTAL DRIFT

The tectonic plates move a few inches (cm) every year because of hot, semi-liquid rocks called magma in a layer under the earth's crust called the mantle. The hot magma and gases churn around, making the continents shift slowly. This process is called continental drift. It is believed that about 200 million years ago all the continents were joined together, but now some have drifted apart.

The San Andreas Fault. In California, the North American and Pacific plates are sliding slowly past each other. Movement along this fault line has caused major earthquakes.

WHAT HAPPENS WHERE PLATES MEET?

Three main things happen when plates meet at plate boundaries, or margins. The plates may move apart, move together, or slide past each other.

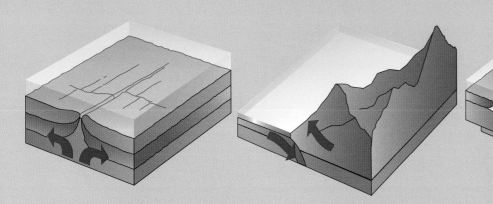

CONSTRUCTIVE BOUNDARY

Most tectonic plates move apart under the oceans. Magma wells up into the gap, then cools and hardens to form lines of mountains under the sea. This is called a constructive boundary, because new crust is formed, or constructed.

DESTRUCTIVE AND COLLISION BOUNDARIES

When tectonic plates move together, the crust may melt and be destroyed, forming a destructive boundary. Sometimes the crust can crumple up to make mountains, forming a collision boundary.

CONSERVATIVE BOUNDARY

Plates can also move sideways against each other. They slide in opposite directions or at different speeds, causing cracks called faults in the plates. These are conservative plate boundaries, because crust is neither gained nor lost.

MAPPING THE PLATES

Earth's crust is made of about 9 large plates and 12 smaller ones. Do some research and see if you can mark the nine large plates on a map of the world.

The movements of Earth's plates create cracks in the crust through which volcanoes can erupt. They also cause earthquakes as the rocks move and jolt past each other, making the ground shake.

On your map of Earth's plates, mark the places where volcanic eruptions and earthquakes usually happen. You could devise a symbol to represent the volcanoes and the earthquakes. What do you notice about the distribution of volcanoes and earthquakes? Volcanoes around the Pacific Plate form a ring that is known as the "ring of fire." Label this on your map, too.

HELPING HAND
You can find blank maps of the world on
www.EnchantedLearning.com/geography/continents/outlinemap

Volcanoes

Volcanoes are formed when magma from Earth's mantle pours out through cracks in Earth's crust. Once the magma is on the surface, it is called lava. Scientists estimate that there are over 1,500 active volcanoes around the globe, which may erupt at any time. A volcano that has not erupted for a long time is called a dormant volcano. An extinct volcano is one that most likely will not erupt again.

WHEN A VOLCANO ERUPTS

Volcanoes are like valves, releasing the pressure of gases that build up beneath Earth's crust. The power of a volcanic eruption and the shape of a volcano depend on the thickness of the magma and the amount of gas trapped in it.

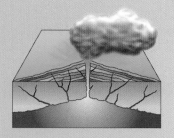

Shield volcano
If the magma is thin and runny, it forms wide, flat shield volcanoes such as the chain of volcanoes that make up the Hawaiian Islands.

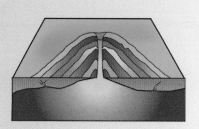

Cinder cone
Thick, sticky magma moves slowly to the surface and cools quickly. This forms a tall, steep-sided cone that widens with every eruption.

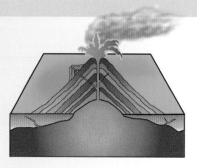

Composite volcano
Magma containing lots of gas bubbles explodes onto the surface. The main cone forms from ash and lava layers with smaller secondary cones on the side.

VOLCANIC PLUGS

When the sides of the volcano have been worn away, the hardened lava in the central vent of a volcano may be left behind as a tall tower of rock. This is called a volcanic plug. There are several examples of volcanic plugs around the world. Try to find pictures of some of them. Start by looking for Devil's Tower in Wyoming, Agathla Peak in Arizona, or the Chapel of St. Michael d'Aguiche, which is on top of a volcanic plug in Le Puy, France.

VOLCANOES DATABASE

Create a database with information about volcanic eruptions throughout the world using sources such as text books, the Internet, newspaper articles, and television documentaries. Collect information such as the location of the volcano, the date of the eruption, the type of eruption, the damage caused to buildings, the effects including mud flows, ash falls, and local climate change, and the number of people killed.

Think carefully about the best way to organize the information. You might choose to record the top 10 biggest volcanic eruptions in history or you may want to look at volcanoes that have erupted recently. Many islands are the tips of undersea volcanoes and most volcanoes erupt under the sea. You could include a column for undersea volcanoes in your database.

PREDICTING ERUPTIONS

About 1 in 10 people live within the "danger zone" of an active volcano. To reduce the number of deaths caused by volcanic eruptions, it is important for scientists to monitor active volcanoes so that they can evacuate people quickly before an eruption occurs. Draw a chart of the different ways scientists monitor volcanoes, such as measuring the tilt of Earth's surface, recording vibrations, measuring gases, and taking the temperature of lava. Today, robots and other remote sensing devices make monitoring volcanoes safer.

Inside the ancient volcanic cone of Mount Vesuvius in Italy.

KEY SKILLS

Collecting, recording, and presenting data

Analyzing information

Doing research

Mountains

Mountains are large landforms with steep sloping sides that are much higher than the land around them. Some geographers say that a mountain must be more than 0.6 miles (1,000 m) high. Mountains make up one fifth of Earth's land area and are also found under the sea. Some mountains stand on their own but most are grouped together to form long mountain ranges or chains that can stretch for hundreds or even thousands of miles.

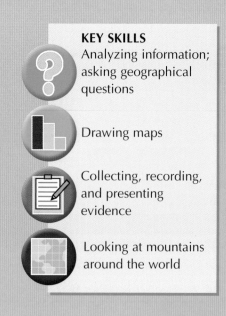

KEY SKILLS

Analyzing information; asking geographical questions

Drawing maps

Collecting, recording, and presenting evidence

Looking at mountains around the world

FOLD MOUNTAINS
Most of the world's mountains are formed as two tectonic plates collide. They are called fold mountains because this movement pushes up the crust in gigantic folds.

BLOCK MOUNTAINS
Sometimes huge slabs of rock are pushed up to form block mountains such as the Sierra Nevada mountain range in eastern California.

DOME MOUNTAINS
Magma rising from inside Earth can force up the crust without breaking through to form dome mountains. The Black Hills in South Dakota, are dome mountains.

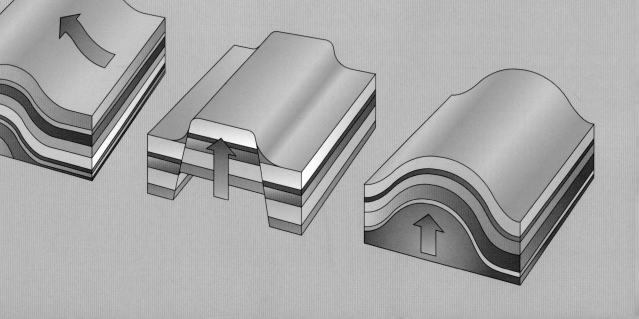

COMPARING MOUNTAINS

Mountains in different parts of the world have different characteristics. Choose two different mountain ranges, one in a less economically developed country (LEDC) and one in a more economically developed country (MEDC).

Draw a map to show the location of each mountain range. Then collect information from as many sources as possible. It is a good idea to decide on a list of features to compare. You may want to consider the following:

- how the mountains formed
- the size of the mountains
- the weather
- the landforms
- the wildlife and the people who live there

PEOPLE WHO LIVE IN MOUNTAIN RANGES

Despite the harsh environment, about 10 percent of the world's population lives in mountainous regions. How do people design their homes to cope with the severe mountain weather? People who live in the mountains are often farmers growing crops such as coffee or raising animals such as yaks or llamas. Some mountain dwellers work in tourism, helping skiers or climbers. How does mountain transportation differ in the two mountain ranges you have studied?

The Himalaya Mountains are fold mountains pushed up by India as it slowly moves north into the rest of Asia.

Earthquakes

Earthquakes occur when energy is suddenly released by plates as they move past each other. They cause the ground to shake violently. The point under the ground where an earthquake starts is called the focus. Vibrations called seismic waves spread out from the focus like ripples from a stone thrown into a pond.

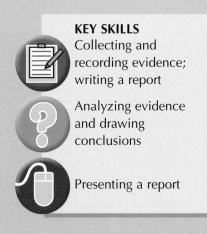

KEY SKILLS
Collecting and recording evidence; writing a report

Analyzing evidence and drawing conclusions

Presenting a report

SEISMIC WAVES

The power of the seismic waves depends on the depth of the focus, the strength of the rocks, and how much the rocks move. Body waves travel inside Earth, while surface waves spread out from the epicenter—the point on the surface directly above the focus of the earthquake.

Most damage occurs at the epicenter of the earthquake. Huge cracks may appear in the land, swallowing cars and buildings.

Large earthquakes can cause homelessness, unemployment, and economic damage across several countries. LEDCs take longer to recover because of their limited resources.

MEASURING QUAKES

The Richter scale measures the amount of energy released by an earthquake. Most serious earthquakes measure a magnitute between five and nine on the Richter scale. The Kashmir/Pakistan earthquake of 2005 measured 7.6 on the Richter scale. Each number on the scale is 10 times more powerful than the one before it and indicates the level of destruction it may have caused.

QUAKE REPORT

Find out as much as you can about a recent earthquake such as the one that hit Kashmir and Pakistan in 2005; the 2001 Gujurat earthquake in India; the Izmit and Istanbul earthquake in Turkey in 1999; or the Kobe earthquake in Japan in 1995. Present your findings as a newspaper report. How did the construction of the buildings affect the amount of damage caused by the earthquake?

Investigate what happened at the time of the earthquake and then look at the time taken to restore the power, water supply, infrastructure such as roads, bridges, and railways, and communications such as telephone lines. Is the country where the earthquake happened an LEDC or an MEDC? How much help did the area receive from its own country or other parts of the world? Has the country made plans to survive any future earthquakes?

The damage from an earthquake in Turkey shows how most buildings can quickly turn to rubble.

Rocks

The shape of landforms partly depends on the type of rocks from which they are formed. There are three main types of rock: igneous, sedimentary, and metamorphic. Each type is formed over time by different processes and has characteristics that affect the landscape in different ways.

The Cliffs of Dover in the United Kingdom (UK) were formed from sediments that built up when this area was covered by water long ago.

DIFFERENT ROCK TYPES

Igneous rocks are formed from magma that cools and hardens, either on Earth's surface or below the ground. There are many examples of igneous formations around the world such as the Giant's Causeway in Northern Ireland and the Devils' Marbles in Australia.

Most sedimentary rocks are formed from small pieces of other rocks called sediments. These are carried away by wind or water and pressed together to form layered rocks. Some sedimentary rocks, such as chalk and limestone, are made of the remains of living creatures. Examples of sedimentary landforms include the Grand Canyon in Arizona, and the Cliffs of Dover in the UK.

Metamorphic rocks are igneous or sedimentary rocks that have been changed by heat, pressure, or both during volcanic activity or tectonic movements. Marble and slate are metamorphic.

THE ROCK CYCLE

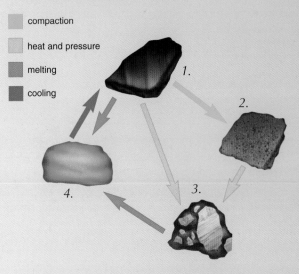

- compaction
- heat and pressure
- melting
- cooling

An igneous rock (1) can be changed first into a sedimentary rock (2) and then into a metamorphic rock (3) before melting to become magma (4) and cooling to become a new igneous rock. This recycling process is called the rock cycle. Many rocks do not complete every stage of the cycle.

ROCK COLLECTION

Collect small pieces of rock to build your own rock collection. Look for rocks, stones, and pebbles in your yard, in the park, or when you visit a beach. If you live in a town, take photographs of the different types of stone used in buildings. Look at the exhibits in some museums to find more ways that rocks have been used in the past. You could also buy rock samples at a museum gift shop or a craft store. Store your rock collection in an old shoebox, using pieces of cardboard to divide the box into sections. Put tissues or paper under your rock samples to protect them. Look in books or ask museum workers to help you learn the names of the rocks. Try to group them in three groups—igneous, sedimentary, and metamorphic rocks.

When you have found the names of your rocks, draw a table similar to the one below. Fill in information on each rock type, including what you discovered about them.

ROCK CHART

Type of rock	Name of rock	How it is used
Igneous	Granite, Basalt, Obsidian, Pumice	Tools and weapons, building stone, roads
Sedimentary		
Metamorphic		

Weathering

The natural breakdown of rocks on Earth's surface is called weathering. The way that weathering changes the shape of the land depends on the climate and the type of rocks. Soft rocks, such as mudstone or chalk, wear away more easily than hard rocks such as granite. Rain in heavy industrial areas often contains higher levels of acidity because of pollution and can wear away stonework on buildings more quickly than cleaner rain.

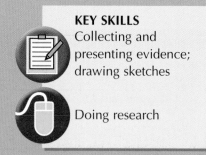

KEY SKILLS
Collecting and presenting evidence; drawing sketches

Doing research

TYPES OF WEATHERING

There are three main types of weathering: physical, chemical, and biological.

Physical weathering happens mainly when rocks heat up and expand by day then cool down and contract at night. This makes the rocks crack and crumble and pieces break or peel off. In cool, moist climates, ice sometimes forms in rock cracks at night, making the cracks wider.

Chemical weathering happens when rocks are eaten away by chemicals such as the acids in rainwater. Chemical weathering often affects limestone rocks, especially along cracks or joints (see pages 24–25). Moist tropical climates encourage fast chemical weathering.

Biological weathering is the breakdown of rocks by plants and animals. Plant roots may be strong enough to enlarge cracks in rocks, and burrowing animals can break up crumbling rocks.

SIGNS OF WEATHERING

See if you can find examples of weathering around you. Most towns have old buildings which often show signs of chemical weathering. Look at the stonework around windows or doors. How have they been affected by chemical weathering? What has happened to the carved details? The same process is responsible for the breakdown of rocks in the natural environment.

Sketch drawings and take photographs to record the examples you find. Use the Internet to find historical pictures of your area to show how parts of buildings have been weathered over time.

COMBINED ATTACK

Landforms are gradually broken down by a combination of different types of weathering. Look at the photographs you took for your study of an old building. Can you see small green or yellow plants growing on the stonework? These are called lichens and many of them release a mild acid that breaks down the surface so that they can cling to walls. Look for lichens on rocks in gardens and parks.

The sandstone rocks of Bryce Canyon in Utah have been weathered and eroded by rain, wind, and snow to form pinnacles called hoodoos.

Erosion

Erosion is the wearing away of land and the removal of weathered or loose material by wind, water, and ice. The wind sweeps up debris and blasts it against the land. Water in rivers carries stones that wear away the riverbed and deposit material downstream. The sea smashes huge waves against cliffs, and ice grinds down rocks.

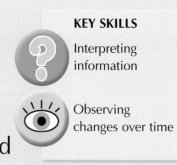

The grass on this path has been slowly worn away by people walking on it. How could it be protected from further erosion?

A SLOW PROCESS

Erosion is a slow process that can only be recorded over a period of time—most changes take years to become obvious.

SPEEDING UP EROSION

The effects of erosion can be sped up, especially through human activity. Look at a well-traveled path at a local park. How has it been affected by people? Look for damage to vegetation and the structure of the top layer of soil. What do you think might happen as the erosion continues? If there is stormy weather, such as heavy rain, strong winds, or floods, you may notice big changes to the landscape in just a few days. Storms can wash away large amounts of soil and can cause landslides, or big pieces of land that slip downhill. Landslides can even make large sections of a cliff collapse.

HELPING HAND
Think about the role that plants play in holding the soil together and reducing the effects of erosion.

THE WATER CYCLE

The shape of landforms changes all the time as rain falls and rivers or oceans carry away pieces of rock. The movement of water between the sky and the surface of Earth forms a continual cycle called the water cycle or the hydrological cycle ("hydro" means water). The amount of water on Earth stays the same—it just moves from place to place.

1. The sun heats water on Earth's surface, turning some of it into water vapor that disappears into the air. This process is called evaporation.

2. If the moist air rises and cools, the water vapor turns back into droplets of liquid water. This is called condensation. The condensed water droplets collect together to make clouds.

3. Rain falls from the clouds back down to Earth's surface. The water flows into streams, rivers, and finally into the sea, completing the water cycle.

Deserts

Deserts cover about one-third of Earth's land surface. There is usually less than 10 inches (25 cm) of rainfall a year in a desert and very few plants survive. High winds, extreme temperature changes, and sudden floods of fast-flowing water erode the landscape. This creates distinctive landforms that are more visible without plants growing over them.

KEY SKILLS

Looking at deserts around the world

Doing research

Designing a poster

This desert landscape of Monument Valley on the border of Arizona and Utah has flat-topped islands of hard rock called mesas and columns of hard rock called buttes. They were probably shaped by water erosion many years ago when the climate in the area was wetter. Softer rocks around the mesas and buttes have eroded.

SHAPING THE LANDSCAPE

Desert sands are picked up by the wind and bounce along the surface in a process called saltation. As the sharp grains of sand bounce along, they hit the rocks and wear them away to form shapes such as arches and pillars. A rock shaped like a mushroom may form if layers of softer rock are worn away near the ground to form a narrow "stalk" and a wide, flat cap of harder rock remains balanced on the top.

DESERT SURVIVAL

Deserts are very hostile environments for wildlife. Plants and animals have to survive scorching hot days and bitterly cold nights. Rain may not fall for months, or even years. Some desert animals do not drink at all. They get all the water they need from their food. Others, such as camels, store fat in their bodies to use as energy when food and water are hard to find. Where do plants such as cacti store water? Why do cacti have spines instead of leaves? Make a poster to show how plants and animals adapt to desert conditions. Research desert wildlife and then create a poster with examples from one desert or from different deserts throughout the world. You may want to concentrate on either plants or animals. You could even choose just one plant, such as a saguaro cactus, or one animal, such as a camel.

SAND DUNES

The wind blows desert sands into mounds called sand dunes. The shape of the dunes depends on the wind speed and direction as well as the amount of sand and plants in the area. The arrows on these illustrations show the direction of the wind.

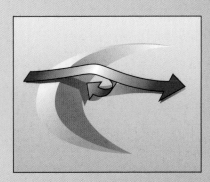

Barchan dunes are formed around obstacles.

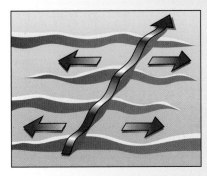

Seif dunes are formed by crosswinds. These dunes are long and gently curving.

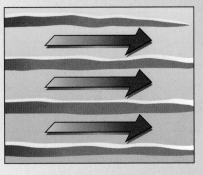

Linear dunes form when the wind blows from one direction.

Star dunes are formed where the wind blows from different directions.

Limestone landscapes

Areas with limestone rocks produce a landscape called karst topography. Very little water flows on the surface of this landscape. Rainwater slowly dissolves the joints in the soft limestone rock to form separate slabs that make a "limestone pavement." The water flows underground through large gaps between the rocks called sinkholes, forming underground rivers.

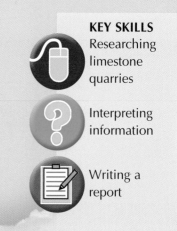

KEY SKILLS

Researching limestone quarries

Interpreting information

Writing a report

This limestone pavement is in Ireland. A limestone pavement is made of blocks of limestone called clints, with cracks between the blocks, called grykes.

Spectacular stalactites and stalagmites in Carlsbad Cavern in New Mexico.

A LIMESTONE CAVE SYSTEM

Rainwater contains acid that dissolves calcium carbonate, the main ingredient found in limestone. Once the water is below the surface and flowing along weak rocks, it hollows out passages and caves. Rainwater can dissolve less than an inch (2.5 cm) of limestone in a year, so a large cave system takes thousands of years to form.

As water seeping through the cave evaporates, it leaves behind drips of watery rock that build up to form stalactites, which hang from the roof of the cave, and stalagmites, which "grow" up from the floor of the cave.

QUARRYING CONFLICT

Limestone is quarried to provide building stone. It is also used as a fertilizer to help crops grow, to make cement, and to make steel.

Limestone quarrying can cause conflicts between the quarry company, the local people, the tourist industry, and environmental groups. Find out some of the arguments for and against quarrying and write a report explaining your findings.

You may find the following arguments for quarrying useful:
- It provides raw materials needed for building and industry

- When the quarry is closed, the hole can be filled with water to make a lake for wildlife and sports

Some of the arguments against quarrying are:
- It produces a lot of noise and dust, which reduces the quality of the environment and keeps tourists from visiting the area
- It increases the amount of traffic including large trucks transporting the stone

HELPING HAND
Log on to
www.goodquarry.com to find
out more about quarries.

Rivers at work

Rivers are natural channels that carry water to other rivers, lakes, or oceans. As rivers flow, they erode the land, carrying material away and depositing it somewhere else. The way that rivers shape the land depends on how fast they flow and the kind of rocks they flow over.

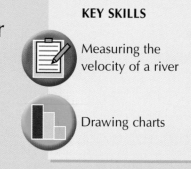
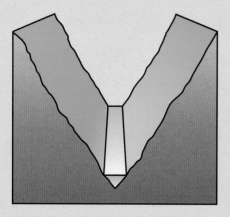

A narrow V-shaped valley near the source of a river.

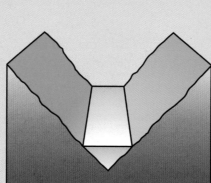

A wider V-shaped valley at the middle of a river.

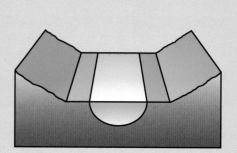

A wide, flat valley near the mouth of a river.

VALLEY SHAPES

At the source of a river, the water cuts into the land to form a narrow, V-shaped valley with steep sides.

In the middle of a river, the water cuts into the land and sideways to form a wider, V-shaped valley. Near the end, or mouth, of a river, the water cuts sideways and also deposits material, forming a wide, flat valley.

A RIVER'S LOAD

The material a river carries is called its load. A river moves, or transports, its load in three main ways:

- Some particles are dissolved in the water
- Fine particles, silt, or clay float in the water and are carried by the water itself.
- Larger particles, such as stones, pebbles, and rocks, roll, slide, or bounce along the bottom of the river.

The shape you see when you look down on a river, such as the one in this satellite photograph, is called its drainage pattern. The main river channel and all the distributaries, or small streams that flow into it (called tributaries), often form a pattern like the branches of a tree.

WARNING! ⚠️
Rivers can be dangerous places. Always follow the safety rules of a teacher or other responsible adult.

HOW FAST DO RIVERS FLOW?

To measure the speed of your local stream or river, see how fast an object floats over a certain distance. Use twigs or stones to mark a distance of 300 feet (91.5 m) along the bank. Drop a stick into the water by one marker and time how long it takes the stick to float to the other marker. Watch how the sticks flow around bends in the stream or river. Do the sticks flow faster in some places than in others?

To calculate the speed, or velocity, of water flow, divide the distance by the time. Measure the speed at different places and make a chart to compare your results. A fairly fast river flows at about 3 miles (5 km) per hour. During a flood, rivers flow much faster, sometimes at 15 miles (25 km) per hour. The speed of a stream or river partly depends on the downhill slope of the riverbed called the gradient. It also depends on the shape of the channel and whether it is rough or smooth.

The upper river

The beginning of a river is called its source. Many rivers have their source in the mountains; others start flowing from a natural hollow in the ground, a lake, a marsh, or a melting glacier.

INTERLOCKING SPURS

At first, the river runs through a deep, narrow valley, winding around areas of hard rock and eroding softer rock. The erosion causes ridges of land to stick out into the river valley. These ridges are called interlocking spurs.

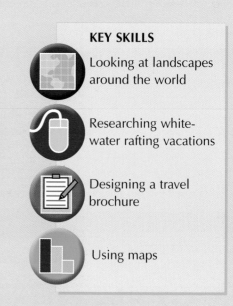
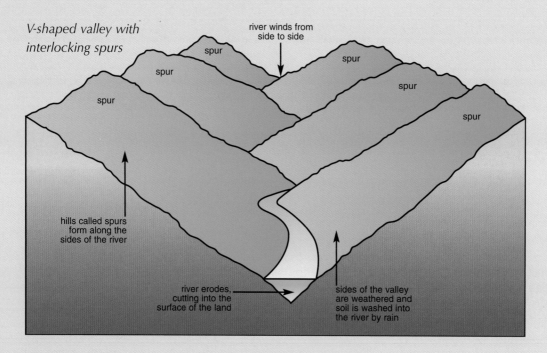

V-shaped valley with interlocking spurs

river winds from side to side

spur

spur

spur

spur

spur

spur

hills called spurs form along the sides of the river

river erodes, cutting into the surface of the land

sides of the valley are weathered and soil is washed into the river by rain

WATERFALLS AND RAPIDS

Waterfalls and rapids are often found near the source of the river. A waterfall occurs where the river flows over a band of hard rock with softer rock on the other side. The softer rock wears away, leaving a large step of rock, over which the water falls in a foaming cascade. The force of the falling water may carve out a deep pool at the base of the waterfall. Rapids form where bands of hard and soft rock break up the flow of the water in a series of small steps.

DESIGN A TRAVEL BROCHURE

The water that flows over rapids in the upper river foams and splashes to make patches of white, frothy water. It is exciting to travel over this "white water" in an inflatable boat or a canoe. This is called whitewater rafting. Design a travel brochure advertising a whitewater rafting adventure. Research whitewater rafting vacations on the Internet or at a travel agency and find out in which parts of the world they take place. Describe and illustrate the river landscape and remember to include a map, details of travel arrangements, and places to stay. How fast does the boat travel? What safety measures must be taken? How does tourist activity such as whitewater rafting affect the river landscape?

The Iguaçu Falls, on the border between Argentina and Brazil, are the widest waterfalls in the world, stretching for about 2 miles (3.2 km). The waterfall system consists of about 275 falls that are up to 230 feet (70 m) tall. More than one million people visit the falls every year.

The middle and lower river

As a river flows farther away from its source, it carries more water and sediment. It also begins to deposit some of its load, creating different features on the landscape.

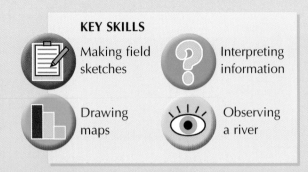

KEY SKILLS

Making field sketches

Interpreting information

Drawing maps

Observing a river

MEANDERS

The course of the river begins to twist from side to side, forming loops or bends called meanders. Sometimes, the river cuts through the narrow neck of land in the middle of a big meander loop. A U-shaped lake is left behind. It is called an oxbow lake because it's shaped like the collar of an ox's yoke.

Eventually, the river flows across a relatively flat plain that is often flooded when the river spills over its banks. When the river reaches the ocean, it slows down and deposits its load. A new piece of land called a delta may form.

The Amazon River meanders across a flat valley in South America. Thick rain forest grows at the edge of the river.

DELTAS

A delta develops when a river drops its sediment faster than the sea can carry it away. The shape of a delta depends on how much water and sediment is in the river and how fast the river is flowing. It also depends on the speed and strength of the waves, currents, and tides in the ocean.

HELPING HAND
The word "delta" comes from the Greek letter Δ (delta) because the ancient Greeks saw that the Nile Delta had the same triangular shape.

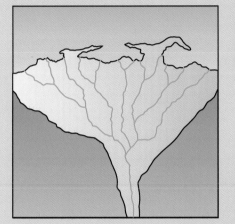

Arcuate (triangle shape) deltas form when the sea has weak waves, currents, and tides. The Nile Delta in Egypt is an arcuate delta.

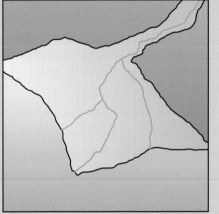

Cuspate (tooth shape) deltas form when the sea has strong waves and currents. The Tiber River delta in Italy is a cuspate delta.

Bird's foot deltas form in calm seawater when the river is carrying a lot of sediment. The Mississippi River delta is a bird's foot delta.

RECORDING RIVERS

If you have a shallow river nearby, you may be able to make a sketch of a meander or part of its course. If you can stand on a hill looking down on the river, it will be easier to see the shape of the river's channel. Look for these features:

- A river cliff—the river flows fastest on the outside bend of a meander and may cut into the banks to form a river cliff.
- A river beach—on the inside bend, the river flows more slowly and deposits some of the material it is carrying. The material may build up to form a river beach.

Identify these features on your sketch using labels. You could also draw a cross section of the riverbed to show clearly how it is shaped by the flowing water.

If you do not live near a river, look at rivers on maps. Identify some of the typical features of a middle or lower stage river, such as wide rivers, flat river valleys, meanders, oxbow lakes, floodplains, and deltas. You could also draw your own map of an imaginary river, showing the different features you would find as you went on a journey from the source of the river to the ocean.

River flooding

River flooding happens when the amount of water in the river suddenly rises and spills over the banks. Floods are often caused by sudden, heavy rainfall or snow rapidly melting in spring. They are also caused by water draining very quickly from towns and cities. Global warming is changing the weather and may cause more floods in the future.

KEY SKILLS

Using the Internet to collect and record information

Analyzing information

Preparing a brochure or poster

The Three Gorges Dam, due to be completed by 2009, will be 1.2 miles (2 km) wide and about 600 feet (183 m) high. It stretches across the world's third longest river, the Yangtze River in China. It will help generate hydroelectricity and reduce flooding.

FLOOD CONTROL

To reduce the damage caused by river flooding, engineers build dams and high riverbanks, called levees, to control the flow of water. This is known as hard engineering. Engineers also make river channels deeper or straighter so that they will carry more water away quickly. These hard engineering solutions change the natural river flow, affecting the environment and often causing flooding problems farther down the river.

Soft engineering solutions tackle flooding using more natural methods. These include planting trees to soak up water, using walls of sandbags to hold back the water, and channeling rainwater into the soil, lakes, or ponds. Predicting floods and preventing new building in areas at risk from flooding is also important.

Dramatic air rescue in Mozambique. Helicopters are sometimes the only way to rescue people trapped by rising floodwaters.

HELPING HAND
This Web site will help you find out more about serious floods.
www.pbs.org/wgbh/nova/flood

AFTER THE FLOOD

A flood disaster can sometimes kill hundreds or even thousands of people. Floodwater, mud, and debris can damage homes, ruin crops, destroy factories, and make it difficult to use roads, railways, or airports. If sewage contaminates the water, then diseases such as cholera can spread quickly, causing many more deaths.

Floods occur in both LEDCs and MEDCs, but the effects are usually worse in LEDCs because the flood warning systems, flood defenses, and flood recovery programs are not as efficient or as well funded. Research a flood, such as the

Mozambique floods in 2000. Find out what happened during the flood and the problems faced by the people of Mozambique afterwards.

Using this information, design a fund-raising brochure or poster to show people the problems faced by flood victims in an LEDC. What kind of pictures would make people give as much money as possible? Give some examples of how the money would be used, such as restoring freshwater supplies or providing medicines. What would be the best ways to deal with floods in the future?

Ice at work

Ice covers about 10 percent of Earth's surface, mainly at the north and south poles and on high mountains. Some land is covered by huge layers of ice called ice sheets, while "rivers" of ice called glaciers sometimes form in mountain valleys. As the ice moves slowly downhill, it drags rocks and pebbles with it and carves the land into new shapes. When the ice melts, it leaves behind ridges, hummocks, and gravel-covered plains, called outwash plains.

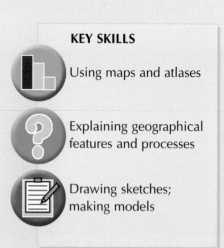

KEY SKILLS

Using maps and atlases

Explaining geographical features and processes

Drawing sketches; making models

LAND SHAPED BY ICE

The enormous size and weight of the glacier ice:

- Carves a V-shaped valley into a straighter U-shape
- Digs out hollows called corries
- Cuts off spurs of land
- Creates egg-shaped mounds called drumlins

When the glacier ice melts and recedes, it:

- Leaves small tributary river valleys "hanging" high above the valley floor
- Leaves behind curved ridges of rock and rubble called moraines, which appear where the sides or end of the glacier used to be
- Leaves behind blocks of melted ice that may form hollows full of water, called kettle holes

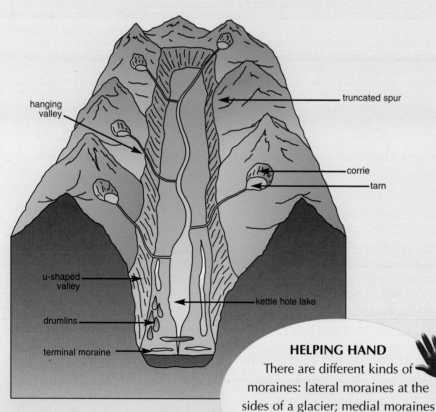

hanging valley

truncated spur

corrie

tarn

u-shaped valley

drumlins

kettle hole lake

terminal moraine

HELPING HAND
There are different kinds of moraines: lateral moraines at the sides of a glacier; medial moraines where two glaciers join; and terminal moraines at the end, or snout, of a glacier.

MAP SPOTTING

Use an atlas or the Internet to find a map of an area featuring glaciers, such as the Columbia Icefield in Canada. Try to identify landforms that were shaped by the power of the ice. Here are some clues to look for:

- Wide, flat valleys with a small river in the middle
- Straight valleys with steep sides
- Side valleys that seem to be cut off where they join the edge of a main valley
- Waterfalls coming from "hanging valleys" down the sides of a main valley
- Small lakes, or tarns, near the top of mountains. These may be where water has collected in a corrie
- A steep peak, called a pyramidal peak, with several corries around it, at the top of a mountain.

Make a drawing or a model to show what the landscape would look like if you visited the area on your map.

A glacier in Alaska. Huge cliffs of ice form on the coast where a glacier or an ice sheet flows into the sea.

Shaping the coast

Where the land meets the sea, the pounding waves create unique coastal landforms. As the waves wash stones and pebbles against the shore, they wear the rocks away. The waves also force air and water into cracks in the rocks, bursting them apart. Water causes a chemical reaction in some rocks that slowly dissolves them. Material produced by all these processes of erosion and the sediment that is deposited on the coast by rivers is transported up, down, and along the coast by waves.

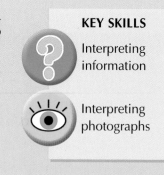

KEY SKILLS

Interpreting information

Interpreting photographs

HOW WAVES FORM

Most waves are caused by the wind blowing across the surface of the ocean to make little peaks of water. Inside each peak, the water moves around in circles. The size and speed of the waves depends on the strength of the wind, the length of time that the wind blows, and the distance the wave travels. Near the coast, the waves slow down in the shallow water, causing the top of the wave to fall and break on the shore.

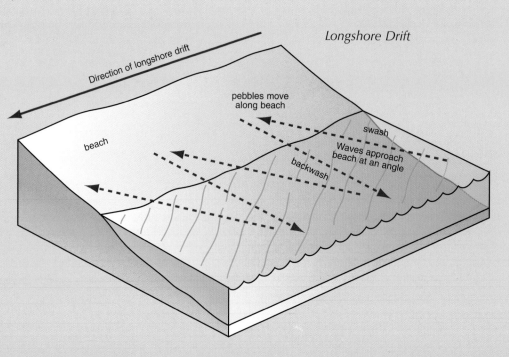

Longshore Drift

Direction of longshore drift

beach

pebbles move along beach

swash

Waves approach beach at an angle

backwash

WAVE MOTION

If waves hit a beach at an angle, they gradually move the beach material sideways in a zig-zag path. This is called longshore drift because the material slowly drifts along the shore.

WAVE WATCHING

On a visit to the coast, watch how the waves pick up sand, rocks, and pebbles and move them around. As the stones and pebbles crash into each other, they break into smaller and smaller pieces. Jagged rocks turn into smooth, round pebbles or eventually small grains of shingle and sand. Collect pebbles from different places on the beach and measure their sizes.

Watch how the waves hit the shore. Do they come straight toward the shore or do they hit at an angle?

In places where longshore drift happens, people sometimes build wooden barriers, called groins, at right angles to the coastline. The groins keep beach material from being carried along the coast so that the beach protects the coast from further erosion.

Use the Internet to find pictures of these wooden barriers and make a sketch of the groins. Why does beach material build up on one side of the groin? What happens further along the coast, where beach material is no longer being deposited because of the groins?

Waves breaking on the shore have immense power and create a foamy white surf. Here, water moves up and down the beach rather than around in circles.

Wearing away coasts

Over long periods of time, wave erosion wears the coast away, forming features such as cliffs, caves, and rock arches. Soft rock wears away faster than hard rock to form bays, and the harder rocks stick out to form points of land called headlands. As the headlands are worn away and material is deposited in the bays, the coastline is gradually smoothed out.

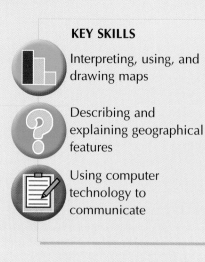

KEY SKILLS

Interpreting, using, and drawing maps

Describing and explaining geographical features

Using computer technology to communicate

The Twelve Apostles are a series of spectacular limestone stacks off the coast of southeast Australia. These tall pillars of rock mark the position of the original coastline, before it was eroded.

WAVE-CUT PLATFORM

Some beaches have a wide, flat area of rock at the base of the cliffs. This is called a wave-cut platform. It forms when waves cut into the bottom of the cliff, making the cliff collapse. Once the waves have removed the cliff material, the flat platform is left behind.

HELPING HAND
You can find out more about erosion on pages 20, 21, 36, and 37 and coastal landforms on pages 40 and 41.

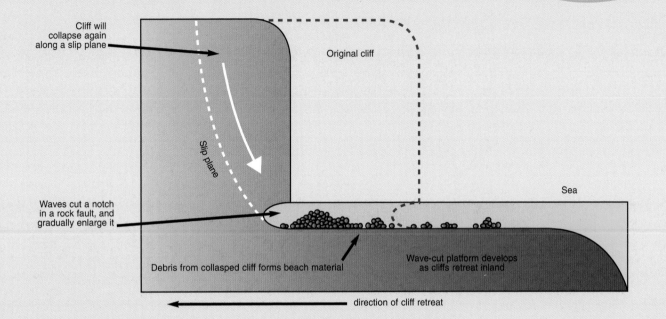

Cliff will collapse again along a slip plane

Original cliff

Slip plane

Sea

Waves cut a notch in a rock fault, and gradually enlarge it

Debris from collasped cliff forms beach material

Wave-cut platform develops as cliffs retreat inland

direction of cliff retreat

FROM CAVES AND ARCHES TO STACKS AND STUMPS

As waves crash against a narrow crack in a headland, they may erode the rock to form a sea cave. If waves cut through a headland, a narrow bridge called a rock arch forms. If the top of the arch collapses, a pillar of rock, called a stack, remains. A stack may collapse into a stump.

COASTAL WALK

Find a map of a coastal area with footpaths and interesting landforms, such as southern Victoria, Australia. Design a brochure showing the coastal walks people might take from a central point such as a parking lot or a tourist information center.

In your brochure, include a map of the area with dotted lines for the different walks. Draw short walks and long walks in different colors and explain how long the walks will take in the key of the map.

At the sides of the map, draw some diagrams showing how the ocean formed the coastal features. Point out any other interesting features, such as offshore islands or nearby hills or towns, that you would be able to see in the distance. Show rest stops with good views and the best places to take photographs.

In a separate box, list safety factors such as:

- Do not go too near the edge of a cliff; it could crumble away
- Cliffs are exposed to the weather; take warm or waterproof clothing with you, if necessary

Building coasts

Some coastal landforms are created when the ocean moves loose material along the shore to form beaches or long ridges of sand and gravel. Larger rocks and pebbles are rolled or bounced along by the waves. Smaller particles of sand and mud float in the water, while salts and other chemicals are dissolved.

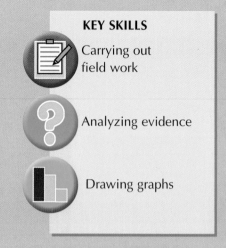

KEY SKILLS

Carrying out field work

Analyzing evidence

Drawing graphs

SPITS AND TOMBOLOS

If there is a break in a coastline, such as where the coast changes direction or at the mouth of a river, longshore drift may push beach material out into the ocean. This forms a long, thin ridge called a spit. The waves may push the end of a spit into a curved shape called a recurved spit.

Sometimes, a spit may connect to an island. This sand or gravel bridge that connects the island to the mainland is called a tombolo.

This is what your finished clinometer should look like. Ask a friend to read the number when the string has stopped swinging. The number is the angle of the slope.

MEASURING BEACHES

On a visit to the beach, measure the angle of slope of the beach and draw a profile of it. The quickest and easiest way to measure the angle of a slope is to use a clinometer. If you do not have a clinometer, you can easily make your own.

MAKING A CLINOMETER

Draw a semicircle on a piece of cardboard and cut it out. Use a protractor to mark degrees on it, with zero degrees in the middle and 90 degrees at each end. Tie a small weight to one end of a short piece of string, and tie the other end to a short, wooden rod. Firmly tape the rod to the straight edge of your paper so that the string swings freely from a point in the middle of the card.

ON THE BEACH

Ask a friend to stand at the top of the beach. Take the clinometer down the slope of the beach and look straight along the wooden rod at your friend's nose. Ask another friend to record the angle where the string crosses the scale. Measure the distance between where the two of you are standing. Then do the same thing at other points further down the slope. Using your results, draw a graph to show the beach profile, with distance along the base of the graph (horizontal axis) and angle of slope up the side (vertical axis).

This series of sandy delta islands is in north Queensland, Australia. You can see a light-colored spit (top, left) being formed by longshore drift.

Managing coasts

About three fourths of the world's people live on or near coasts. Natural processes of coastal erosion often threaten their homes and livelihoods. Coastlines can also be damaged by storms, hurricanes, or natural disasters such as tsunamis. Global warming is causing water levels to rise, putting more coastlines at risk from flooding in the future.

KEY SKILLS

Interpreting information

Writing a formal letter

PROTECTING THE COAST

Coastal communities try to protect themselves from the wind and the waves in a variety of ways. Hard engineering solutions to flooding and erosion use barriers to hold back the sea or absorb the energy of the waves. The barriers include fences called groins (see pages 36 and 37), seawalls, revetments (slatted barriers, left), and gabions (steel mesh cages full of boulders). These barriers cost a lot of money and are only a temporary solution to the problem. They often increase erosion further along the coast.

Soft engineering solutions involve building and conserving beaches, dunes, marshes, and mangrove swamps near the coast to increase the natural protection along the shoreline. The coast is allowed to erode naturally, and houses are moved as necessary or built further inland.

(LEFT) Revetments such as these at Prestatyn in northern Wales help reduce the force of the waves and reduce coastal erosion. They protect the coast more than a seawall, but they upset the natural beauty of a coastal area.

LIVING NEAR A CLIFF

Imagine you live in a house near the edge of a cliff. The sea is eroding the cliff, and the edge of the cliff is now only 100 feet (30 m) away from your home. Houses near yours have already fallen down the cliff. Write a letter for your local politicians asking them to do more about protecting the coast. What points would you make in the letter?

Think about how much coastal defenses would cost. Do you think a hard or a soft engineering solution would best solve your problem?

This house has become a victim of coastal erosion and people can no longer live in it.

What arguments would you use to persuade the politicians to act quickly? Would the defenses reassure tourists and help attract them to the area? Are there any public buildings, such as schools, churches, or libraries, close by?

Include some photographs, maps, and diagrams to show how bad the problem is. Would you be prepared to move if the cliff could not be protected against the sea? Ask if the local government would be prepared to pay you for having to move.

Glossary

Cholera
A severe, life-threatening bacterial infection of the small intestine, usually caused by contaminated water or food.

Clinometer
A device for measuring the angle and height of a slope.

Continental drift
The way the continents slowly drift around the globe because of powerful forces deep inside the earth.

Contour line
A line on a map connecting places that are the same height above sea level.

Corrie
A deep hollow scraped out by the ice at the start of a glacier.

Delta
A mass of alluvium (muddy river sediment), which is often triangular in shape, found at the mouth of a river.

Deposit
When a river or the sea puts sediment down.

Drumlin
A smooth mound of glacial debris, usually shaped like an egg. Drumlins often occur in groups.

Epicenter
The point on the earth's surface directly above the focus of an earthquake.

Erosion
The loosening of weathered material and the carrying away of this material by the wind, water, or ice.

Floodplain
The wide, flat valley floor, often found in the lower course of a river, which is often flooded by river water.

Global warming
A gradual increase in the average temperature of the earth's atmosphere.

Groins
Fence-like structures on a beach that trap sand or pebbles and reduce longshore drift.

Hard engineering
Building structures to control geographical processes, such as river flooding or coastal erosion.

Igneous rock
A rock formed when magma cools and hardens underground or lava cools and hardens on the earth's surface.

Lava
Molten rock on the earth's surface.

Less economically developed country (LEDC)
A country in which the majority of the population lives in poverty. These countries tend to be mainly rural, but often their cities are growing fast.

Longshore drift
The movement of sediment along the shore when waves strike the shore at an angle.

Magma
Rock in a hot, molten state deep below the earth's surface.

Meanders
Large bends in a river, formed by erosion and deposition.

Metamorphic rock
A rock formed when igneous or sedimentary rocks are altered by heat, pressure, or both.

Moraines
Piles of boulders, rocks, pebbles, and soil carried along by a glacier or left behind when a glacier has melted.

More economically developed country (MEDC)
A country with much greater wealth per person and more developed industry than a less economically developed country.

Mouth
Where a river enters the ocean.

Sediment
Rock debris that is carried or deposited by water, ice, or wind.

Sedimentary rock
A layered rock that forms from the debris of other rocks and the remains of plants or animals.

Silt
Tiny grains or particles of rock.

Soft engineering
Using natural environmental processes to cope with geographical problems, such as flooding or coastal erosion.

Spit
A finger-like ridge of sediment joined to coastal land at one end but extends out into open water.

Stack
A tall pillar of rock left behind when the sea erodes a cliff.

Tombolo
A sand bridge linking an island with the mainland.

Tsunami
A huge sea wave triggered by an undersea earthquake.

Weathering
The gradual breakdown of rocks on the earth's surface by the weather, plants and animals, or chemicals.

Web sites

http://earth.google.com
Download free aerial photographs and the corresponding map of any location in the world.

http://library.thinkquest.org/17457/english.html
Well-illustrated site, with information about the Earth's tectonic plates and a volcanoes database.

http://en.wikipedia.org/wiki/Mountain
Facts and figures about mountains, together with photographs of mountains around the world.

http://quake.usgs.gov
Maps, research, preparing for earthquakes, the latest quake information and links to other sites.

http://ga.water.usgs.gov/edu/earthglacier.html
Water science for schools, including the water cycle, glaciers and icecaps, glaciers in the landscape, and Ice Ages.

www.enchantedlearning.com/geography/rivers
Information on how rivers work, major rivers of the world (including maps), U.S. rivers, and the water cycle.

www.irn.org
Web site for the International Rivers Network, which protects rivers and defends the rights of people who depend on them.

http://www.ga.gov.au/education/facts/landforms
Information on Australian landforms, including Uluru, mountains, rivers, islands, waterfalls, and deserts.

Note to parents and teachers:

Every effort has been made to ensure that these Web sites are suitable for children, that they are of the highest educational value, and that they contain no inappropriate or offensive material. However, because of the nature of the Internet, it is impossible to guarantee that the contents of these sites will not be altered. We strongly advise that Internet access be supervised by a responsible adult.

Index